STARTING WITH
TROPICAL FISH

Bernd Greger

Translated by Astrid Mick
Edited by David Alderton

Contents

Introduction

If you have ever visited a large public aquarium, you, like millions of other visitors, have probably been impressed by this silent underwater world. Apart from beneath the water, nowhere else can fish and aquatic plants be better observed than in an aquarium. This experience has developed into one of the most popular hobbies – that of the aquarist.

A wide variety of tropical fish and plants that are particularly suitable for aquariums, many of which have been specially bred for this purpose, are now available through the aquarist trade. The requisite equipment and accessories have reached quite an advanced stage technologically and are reasonably priced. Thus equipped, it is now possible for us to observe an underwater habitat, and all that goes on in a world alien to us, right in our living-rooms. This experience, which would otherwise only be available to a fully equipped diver, is now available to everyone.

This book is intended to encourage you to set up and equip your own aquarium. Its aim is to guide your first steps in aquarium-keeping and to prevent any of the early disappointments and failures which can spoil your enjoyment of this hobby. To those who have gathered some experience with aquariums already, it offers an opportunity to check and improve upon the measures of care that they have undertaken so far. Further details and information can be obtained from the specialist literature.

A landscape aquarium at the Berlin Zoo.

Previous pages: The harlequin fish (Rasbora heteromorpha) is a shoal fish.

Why not set up your own aquarium?

The increasing numbers of people on this planet and, inevitably, the increasing stress inflicted upon the environment have focused our attention on processes that occur in nature. While, years ago, an aquarium was simply a container in which to keep fish, nowadays it has become a carefully designed 'green ecosystem'. Even for the novice, it is now no problem to set up and maintain an aquarium.

The technology at our disposal today enables us to simulate almost all the climatic and habitat-related processes that occur in the waters of the world:

- The temperature of the aquarium water can be raised or lowered.
- The lighting can be varied in intensity by means of dimmer switches and switched on and off by automatic timers.
- Water can be kept clean by filtration systems.
- Optimum water-quality values can be maintained by electronically controlled devices.
- Food and fertilizer doses can be automated.

Today, aquarium tanks are manufactured in all shapes and sizes, and have been made more resistant to water damage. Electrical safety has also been considerably improved.

Finally, the multitude of fish and plants available from the aquarist trade makes it possible to stock a variety of species. An aquarium well stocked with plants, properly illuminated and with a wisely chosen selection of fish, will offer enjoyment, variety and relaxation from everyday stress.

Choosing a tank

Nowadays, aquarium tanks no longer have frames but consist of glass panels joined together with silicon sealant. Tanks of standard dimensions (length × width × height), e.g. 90 × 30 × 30 cm (36 × 12 × 12 in) are particularly reasonable in price. With glass less than 12 mm (1/2 in) thick, these tanks are quite heavy, even when empty, and so require a secure base. If you wish, you can have a tank made to your own specifications but this, of course, will be more expensive. Tanks made of moulded transparent plastic are lighter but scratch more easily.

When you rinse out the tank before setting up your aquarium, make very sure that the special, non-toxic silicon sealant used to glue the glass panels together is watertight. Its opacity will prevent algae penetrating the strips of sealant and destroying them. The thickness of sealant should be about 1 mm (1/16 in) for small tanks with a capacity of up to 100 l (20 gall).

In progressively larger tanks, the water pressure increases correspondingly and the glued edges will become subjected to a correspondingly greater stress. In very large tanks, from about 500 l (110 gall) upwards, thick, sausage-like ribbons of sealant are necessary to provide greater safety.

The long panels of large tanks need to have strips of glass glued onto the insides horizontally, as supporting bars, to give them better stability. These stabilizers will serve as a support for the cover panel which runs across the top of the tank. The glass strips should be a little shorter at the corners to enable the cables and tubing to be installed. Tanks longer than 1 m (40 in) should have additional cross-reinforcements glued between the front and back panels. If you purchase a reputable make of tank, the unit will have been designed with such considerations in mind.

Before setting up an aquarium you should first determine exactly where you are going to put it. Make absolutely sure that the total weight is supported evenly on the base bearing the tank. A firm plate of polystyrene placed beneath the tank will make up for any irregularities in the surfaces. Otherwise, the increased water pressure at vulnerable points will force the sealant apart.

The best position for your aquarium

Water is heavy: 1 l weighs 1 kg (1 gall weighs 10 lb). You can easily work out the volume of water that your tank will hold by multiplying together the length, width and height of the tank in centimetres and dividing the total by 1,000 to give the figure in litres. Therefore, the weight of water contained in a 120 × 30 × 38 cm (48 × 12 × 15 in) tank will amount to 136 kg (2³/₄ cwt). Allow about 150 kg (3 cwt) for the glass, 50 kg (1 cwt) for the substrate and a further 150 kg (3 cwt) or so for the stand beneath and you will not be far off 500 kg (¹/₂ ton).

Below: *Angelfish (Pterophyllum spp.) move gracefully through their aquarium.*

It is therefore important to check the strength and carrying capacity of the floor of the room, and the positions of beams. It is a good idea to place the tank against a wall, preferably exactly on top of the load-bearing beams. These kinds of weights are not that extraordinary compared with that of a full bookcase or a piano.

An aquarium is best sited in the eye-catching position directly opposite the entrance to the room. If the bottom of the tank is at a height of about 60–80 cm (24–32 in) and the aquarium is surrounded by seating, it will provide a focus of attraction in the living-room.

If you are thinking of using an aquarium as a room-divider remember that the cross-lighting falling from different parts of the room will, to an observer, dull the colours of the fish and plants.

The most outstanding effect can be achieved in the evening by switching off all other lights so that only the light from the aquarium illuminates the room.

These fish and plants form an almost perfect environment in an aquarium.

Basic equipment for your aquarium

The following items will be needed for a first aquarium with a capacity of about 100 l (20 gall.):

- **Stand or base**
- **Tank**
- **Heater** and **thermostat**
- **Filtration system**
- **Lighting system**
- **Decoration** (roots, stones) and **substrate** for the bottom.
- Accessories, e.g. a **water conditioner** to neutralize chlorine and similar chemicals, and a **net**
- **Plants**, either living or plastic
- **Fish** plus suitable **food** for them

Why this equipment is necessary and its role in the aquarium are explained in the following pages. You should aim to enjoy your aquarium and this will require expenditure on equipment, as well as on the occupants of the tank.

For example, if you try to skimp on illumination, you will never be able to watch your fish properly and the plants will die back; if the tank is aerated only by means of an air-stone, the water may soon be affected badly by algal growth.

Cleaning and caring for your aquarium

The weekly cleaning of an aquarium should never be a major operation, unlike the annual 'spring-clean', in which all the equipment, including the gravel on the bottom and the plants, is removed from the tank and washed and cleaned.

This would so disrupt the environmental balance in the tank, which only gradually becomes established, that algae would grow even faster than before and disease might break out among the fish. It is much more sensible to do a weekly clean with a gravel-cleaning siphon that will suck water out of the aquarium as well as thoroughly cleaning the substrate. At the same time, wipe off the inside of the front glass panel with a special magnetic glass-cleaner (see p. 23). Remove all water spots (caused by hard-water deposits) on the outside of the glass. Change the filter medium as necessary.

Once you have discovered which doses of fertilizer best encourage plant growth, you need only shorten the shoots of plants now and again. Shoots that are too long should be cut back to about two-thirds their length and the tops pushed into the substrate. The original plant can remain in the aquarium and new shoots will grow from it.

You should be able to maintain a properly equipped aquarium for years with only minimal effort. Further water-care measures are discussed on pp.19–20

Decorating your aquarium

Garden-lovers will spend a lot of time and effort in planning and maintaining their ornamental gardens. Walls, paths, lawns, bushes and trees are the means of creating a decorative garden. The same kind of care is required when equipping an aquarium. In neither case are you creating a genuinely natural habitat, although you will be able to create a harmonious 'landscape picture', according to your taste, by the judicious arrangement of the elements. With respect

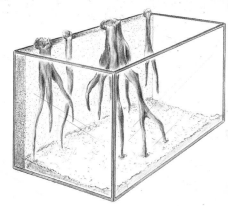

Decoration using sections of bogwood root. A sturdy foam panel serves as a background.

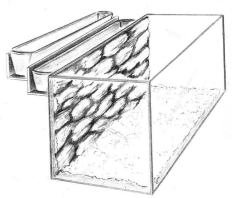

The back panel can be disguised with decorative plastic material. There is room for two plant troughs behind it.

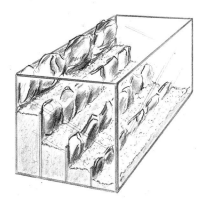

An aquarium landscape can be created with pieces of slate. The different steps are built with the help of strips of glass.

to an aquarium landscape, everything you create will have 'bonsai dimensions'. Divers, ruined castles and plastic fish or plants should have no place in this scheme!

Only choose **rocks** that will not dissolve in the water. Avoid those containing limestone for this reason, unless you are keeping fish that require hard-water conditions, because limestone is soluble and will affect the chemistry of the water. Avoid stacking rocks on top of each other because these structures may collapse with devastating results. Forming the gravel on the bottom into little hillocks is also a waste of time because water movement, produced by the action of the filter system and the movement of the fish, will soon render the surface even again.

All objects destined to be put in the tank should be large enough to be removed easily from the tank for cleaning purposes as they will all provide a good substrate for algae to flourish. For the same reason you should not fix objects permanently to the inside of the glass panels.

The special **wood** (bogwood) sold for use in aquariums has a high density that prevents it from floating in water and pieces can be placed in suitable positions in the tank. Soak the wood thoroughly first to clean it. **Imitation roots** and **stones** made of ceramic or plastic are also available.

Filling the tank with water

First **rinse** the tank to ensure that it is clean. A clean watering-can, which has never contained chemicals, may be used for this purpose.

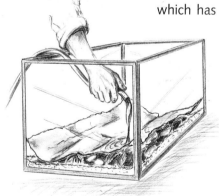

If you do not want to use a bucket to remove the water from the tank, you can siphon it out. Take a hose-pipe or length of tubing and fill it with water from the tap, closing off the ends with your fingers. Place one end in the tank below the water surface and the other in a container, below the level of the tank, into which the water can drain away, releasing your fingers as you do so. Alternatively, you can use a battery-powered siphon which may help to clean the gravel as well. (see also p.9.)

Care is required when filling the tank so that the contents are not churned up.

If you are using an **under-gravel filter**, place it on the floor of the tank. Before pouring the aquarium **gravel** over the filter, rinse it thoroughly in a colander to ensure that no scum forms on the surface once the tank is full and that the water remains clear when the tank is eventually filled.

When **filling the tank**, direct the stream of water onto a root, stone or even a saucer, temporarily placed on the floor, to prevent the water from churning up any gravel or other objects that have already been installed in the tank.

To provide a **background** it is sufficient to stick black card to the outside of the side and rear panels of the tank with sticky tape. Card can also be shaded to produce an illusion of depth. Plastic sheets depicting various underwater scenes, available from aquarist stores, can also be fixed to the outside of the tank. Constructing a decorative back 'wall' to place inside the tank is rather more complicated. The illustrations on p. 9 show several examples of this.

Plants should not be inserted into the gravel until the tank is about three-quarters full of water. They should be removed from their pots and the roots should be cut back to a few centimetres. Never allow the leaves to dry out before planting. It is always a good idea to use aquarium plants that grow as quickly as possible. It is also preferable to allow the plants two weeks to adjust before putting any fish in the tank.

Red phantom tetra (Megalamphodus sweglesi); male in the foreground.

*Java fern (*Microsorium pteropus*) will even withstand the attacks of perches.*

Suitable substrates for aquarium plants

Although aquarium plants absorb a certain proportion of their nutrient requirements directly from the water, the substrate can also play a significant role in their nourishment. Fertilizers, supplied when the tank is being set up or inserted into the substrate during everyday running, will aid their growth. More details can be found on p. 22.

The substrate covering the tank floor will also serve as decoration. To simulate the situation in the wild, it is a good idea to choose natural-coloured gravel with a diameter of 2–10 mm ($^1/_{16}$–$^1/_2$ in), if it is available. If the substrate is too fine, there will be insufficient oxygen for the colonies of beneficial bacteria to develop and these are essential to the function of the undergravel filter (see also p. 18).

The substrate at the bottom of the tank is essential to the proper functioning of an undergravel filter.

You must on no account use peat or soil from the garden for this purpose because the high proportion of organic matter which it contains will decompose, resulting in the accumulation of gases; the algae population will explode, taking over the tank, and the plants will then die.

Safety and electrical appliances

The hairdryer-in-the-bath-tub as the classic murder weapon is only too familiar from murder mysteries on television, so everyone is probably aware of the dangers of handling electrical equipment around water. While aquarists will not take a bath in their aquarium, they may occasionally put their hands in the aquarium water. If a heating unit is broken or an aquarium lamp falls into the water, there is a high likelihood of sustaining an **electric shock**.

For this reason, efforts have been made to produce small electrical appliances which run at a low voltage and so are less dangerous. These appliances have a **transformer** inserted between them and the dangerous mains voltage at the electric socket.

Additional safety is ensured by the presence of a **fault-current switch.** All electrical appliances used in or around aquariums should bear a recognized **safety mark**. The aquarist trade or a consumer advice centre can give you the relevant information on these but always switch off and disconnect electrical equipment before placing your hand in the water. Obviously you should buy a heater which switches off automatically when the water reaches the desired temperature – otherwise there is a danger of overheating.

Great care should be taken when handling electrical equipment near water!

Use of lighting to simulate tropical conditions

Special fluorescent lamps have been designed for illuminating aquariums, and they are cheap and easy to operate. Two or three

Open aquariums can be equipped with pendent lamps.

13

arranged in a row will enable an almost even illumination of the surface. This form of lighting is mounted inside the aquarium cover (hood or reflector) and must be protected against splashes of water. It can be placed directly on top of the aquarium, above the protective glass or plastic panel which forms part of the unit.

The **colour of the light** can be the same in all the lamps or can be varied according to your taste. Ordinary flourescent lights will have only a very slight influence on the growth of plants. If you wish, you can experiment with fluorescent lamps that have been specially devised to enhance plant growth. The spectrum of their light output is very similar to that of sunlight.

The right period of illumination has proven to be 10–12 hours daily. Generally, fish will soon get used to the sudden switching on or off of the lamps.

In order to achieve an even illumination, tanks are now being constructed in standard sizes which correspond to the lengths of the different fluorescent lamps. The use of two fluorescent lamps for an aquarium up to 40 cm (16 in) high is often recommended. Another lamp should be added for every further 10 cm (4 in) height. If the lamps are suspended above the aquarium, rather than being placed directly on top of it, you can increase the intensity of the illumination by adding another lamp or setting up reflectors.

The shield on the right in front of the lamps will prevent an observer from being seen by the fish.

Be prepared to change the lamps even before they have ceased to work, especially if you have plants in the aquarium. The light output of the lamps de-creases progressively and this can adversely affect the growth of plants. Manufacturers may recommend replacing tubes annually.

Checking the water

Water chemistry will differ according to where you live. Water hardness is one important feature. Some fish, such as tetras, generally prefer to live in soft water, in rivers often swollen by rain water. At the other extreme, cichlids from the Rift Valley of Africa require hard water, containing salts dissolved from the rock lining of the lakes. Avoid adding any limestone to your aquarium, in the form of gravel or rocks, unless, you want hard water conditions.

The other important aspect of water chemistry is its pH reading, which measures the relative acidity. Water with a pH reading below 7 is acid, while above 7 is alkaline. PH7 itself is neutral. The further that the reading diverges from pH7, the greater the degree of acidity or alkalinity

Tap water generally has a pH reading of between 7 and 8. This suits most fish, although there are exceptions. The spectacular **discus** (*Symphysodon aequifasciata*) typically require more acidic conditions if they are to thrive, while conversely, Rift Valley cichlids should be kept in more alkaline water.

The correct water temperature will help make both fish and plants feel comfortable.

Fish can adapt gradually to changes in water chemistry, but sudden shifts can leave them vulnerable to illness, and may even prove to be fatal. Buying fish is therefore a good idea as they should already be at least partially acclimatised to the local water conditions. Further changes may then have to be made to encourage breeding.

Regular monitoring of the water chemistry is important to the continued well-being of your fish. This can be carried out quite easily using special test kits from your local aquatic shop, and alterations to the condition of the water can also be made when necessary. This can be done in a variety of ways, depending on the change required.

16

Some chemicals in the water can be toxic to fish. This is why it is especially necessary to use water conditioner when setting up a new tank or carrying out a partial water change, to eliminate chlorine or similar chemicals added for purification purposes.

Maintaining the water at the optimum temperature

The problem with keeping animals and plants which are native to temperate regions lies in maintaining the aquarium water at a low enough temperature: in the average living-room it will become too warm.

Tropical fish and plants are therefore ideal because they can cope with much higher temperatures. In addition, a much greater variety of species and colours is found among tropical fish and many fully grown tropical species are much smaller than temperate species. The tropical aquarium is, therefore, an ideal way of observing this underwater world.

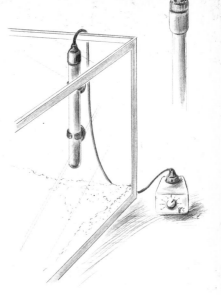

The wattage of this heating unit should be kept as low as possible.

Our homes are so much better heated these days that just a low wattage will be sufficient to adjust the temperature of the aquarium water to that found in the tropics.

At an average room temperature of about 21°C (70°F), an output of 30 W will be sufficient to heat 100 l (20 gall) of water. If you are in any doubt, always opt for the lower wattage figure because the life expectancy of heating systems which are constantly being switched on and off will be reduced.

The simplest way to maintain the desired water temperature in an aquarium is by means of a thermostatically controlled **heaterstat** that can be fixed vertically to a corner of the tank by means of suction cups. A tiny lamp in the unit shows when the heater is in operation. A small screw can be adjusted to regulate the temperature. The temperature can be monitored via a thermometer, which should be sited at a reasonable distance from the heating unit, until the desired level is reached.

Heating mats that are laid immediately beneath the floor of the tank can be useful for larger fish, e.g. cichlids, which may attack a heaterstat or lay their eggs on the exposed heating unit, where they are likely to be destroyed. The water temperature should be kept at an average of about 25°C (77°F).

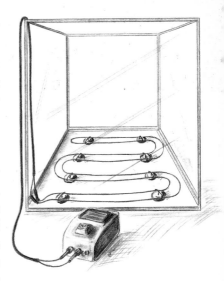

Here is a low-wattage aquarium heating system that functions as under-floor heating.

When positioning your aquarium, you should avoid, as far as possible, sites near any source of heat (a radiator or fire), draughts (doors), natural light (windows), noise or vibration (stereo equipment, a television or 'through traffic').

Some plant species, e.g. *Cryptocoryne* spp., or species of fish such as the discus (*Symphysodon aequifasciata*), may benefit from slightly higher temperatures.

A filter is essential

The water in an aquarium should never look cloudy and no floating substances should be present. An aquarium will only look attractive if these rules are followed. In order to achieve this quality, you will need a well-functioning filter that can process the volume of water in question.

When its effectiveness begins to deteriorate, the filter sponge will need cleaning. This is a minor operation – as the sponge can easily be pulled out easily and then rinsed clean. Use water from the tank for this purpose because the chlorine in tapwater may adversely affect the beneficial bacteria present in the sponge.

Under-gravel filters – perforated plastic sheets of different sizes – can be operated by means of an air-pump. However, their effectiveness is dependent on them being covered with a filter bed of gravel. You may wish to use another type of filter as well. One disadvantage of air-pumps is worth mentioning: the sound of the vibrations can be quite disturbing and may be difficult to ignore. Be sure to choose a design that is quiet when in operation.

Box-type filters are now available in the form of either internal filters, which can be placed directly in a corner of the tank, or external filters, which are typically larger and need to be positioned somewhere outside the tank.

All power filters that are operated by an internal motor are easy to use and relatively inexpensive. In the simplest units of this type, the water flows through a filtering medium, usually an artificial foam sponge, which retains solid particles of debris and absorbs pollutants, after which the purified water runs back into the aquarium.

In the case of **external filters** that are powered by rotary pumps, the filter medium is held in a container beneath the pump. A thin sheet of specially woven nylon or cotton fabric placed on top of this will filter out coarser floating particles. Beneath this, should be a layer of a porous substance, e.g. one of the many fine filter media obtainable from specialist retailers. Because the filter medium is extremely porous it has a very large surface area

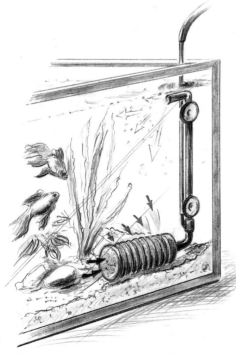

The filter medium in this internal filter consists of an artificial sponge that can be removed for cleaning.

and this encourages colonization by bacteria. It is the bacteria that break down most invisible harmful substances by a biological process. This type of filter system must be kept running non-stop so that the aerobic bacteria do not die through lack of oxygen.

Whatever type of filter system you use, the water should always flow back into the aquarium just beneath the surface of the water. Avoid creating a strong current which will be disruptive in the aquarium, especially to plants and less active fish. The oxygen level in the water can be improved by running an air-stone in conjunction with the air-pump.

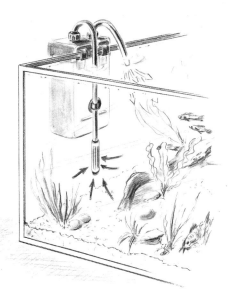

Keeping the water clean and clear

Even the best-working, best-maintained filter system cannot absorb all the harmful substances from the water and even water that looks completely clear may still be severely chemically polluted by the colourless secretions of the fish. This is why, as well as maintaining water quality with filters, you should also undertake a regular partial water change, using fresh tapwater. The tapwater should first be treated with a water conditioner to counteract any chlorine or similar substances added at the water purification works; these are potentially toxic to fish.

An external power filter incorporating a pump that can be attached directly to the outside of a panel of the tank.

A fortnightly change of one third of the water in the aquarium is recommended so that the fish do not suffer from a build-up of their own waste products. Check that the temperature of the fresh water is similar to that of the water in the aquarium.

A gravel-cleaner and tubing is excellent for sucking out mud and debris and for the partial changing of water.

Mixing cold tapwater with the warm water in the tank is not a good idea because, during the process of heating up the water, carbon dioxide, which is so essential for aquarium plants during the hours of daylight, will be driven out.

At the same time as carrying out a partial water change, use a gravel-cleaner to siphon out any sediment that has been deposited on the aquarium floor.

Some gravel-cleaners have a pump in the suction head to start the water flow. If not, first fill both the suction head of the gravel-cleaner and the tubing with water, making sure that the end of the tubing is firmly closed with your finger. Hold the opening of the suction head beneath the water surface and place the end of the tubing in a bucket, releasing your finger so that the water begins to run out. Never be tempted to suck water through to create a flow. This is dangerous because of the potentially harmful bacteria in any water which you may inadvertently swallow. A battery-powered siphon may be a better option.

After a water change, the fish usually display an improved appetite and will often spawn immediately afterwards. This is clear proof of the benefits of a regular partial water change.

The tiny bubbles of oxygen that form on the undersides of the leaves indicate that the aquarium plants are also feeling the benefit of the water change. Carbon dioxide, introduced in the tapwater, stimulates plant growth. Thus the aquarium plants, as well as the fish, thrive as a result of regular partial water changes.

In some regions, tapwater will not be suitable for sensitive tropical fish or aquarium plants. Your local water supplier should be able to give you precise details about the chemical composition of your water, such as its hardness.

In addition, you should be able to measure a number of water-quality factors yourself. Special reagents have been developed for this purpose. Attempts to change the water chemistry should only be undertaken after consulting an expert and studying the relevant reference material.

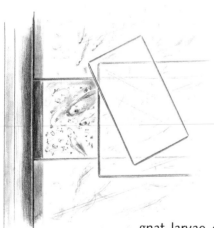

The habitual feeding spot in an aquarium is easy to cover over with a properly cut piece of glass.

Feeding your fish

Nourishment is a basic requirement of all living creatures and tropical fish are no exception. The most basic rule is to watch your fish to see whether they aretaking sufficient nourishment. You should be concerned if they keep spitting out food yet still seem hungry. This could be a sign of illness or it could just mean that you will have to find out which foods your fish prefer.

If they refuse to eat the food you supply, you will first of all have to take recourse to **live food**, as the hopping about and wriggling of water fleas or gnat larvae can stimulate the fish's appetite quite considerably. However, there is a risk of introducing diseases to the aquarium with live food of unknown origin.

Healthy fish will soon learn where food appears in the aquarium and will swim there whenever they glimpse movement nearby. This is why they should always be fed in the same place.

Nevertheless, seeing the fish swim to this position in the aquarium does not mean that you should automatically feed them. Most

Different species of aquarium plants make different demands on their environment and these must be taken into consideration when equipping the tank. Here is a densely planted Dutch aquarium (see also p. 32).

beginners make the mistake of giving far too much food, thus running the risk of polluting the water. It is quite sufficient to offer the fish as much food as they can eat within a few minutes just twice a day. If they are not fed occasionally it will not matter.

The quality of the food is more important than the quantity. This is why you should change the food from time to time. **Frozen live food** has proved to be excellent and a wide range of food species can be obtained from aquarist stores. It needs to be thawed out before being offered to the fish. **Dry food**, in the form of flakes or granules, is obtainable for particular species of fish, e.g. the discus (*Symphysodon aequifasciata*), or for general feeding purposes.

The optimum diet will comprise a constant rotation of live food, deep-frozen food and dry food. This means offering the fish all the types of food available in turn.

Some aquarium plants can be fertilized directly at the roots.

While you are on holiday or away, you can use an **automatic feeding device** which will dispense a small amount of dry food every day. Alternatively special **holiday blocks** are available that dissolve slowly and dispense food gradually over a weekend or longer period of time. This is probably better than asking a neighbour to feed your fish; he or she might give the fish far too much food from a misguided, well-meaning intention. As a result, you may have to refit the aquarium completely on your return because the floor of the tank will be covered in a thick layer of rotten fish-food. This is likely to pollute the water, overload the filter system and be potentially fatal to the fish.

It is preferable to allow your fish to go hungry for a few days. This is not a problem for well-nourished fish because, in the wild,

they seldom obtain a regular meal every single day and some will eat algae, like that growing in the aquarium.

Feeding your aquarium plants

It is customary to repot your ornamental plants, e.g. those on a windowsill, every spring. This is necessary because the plants require more energy when temperatures begin to rise and the sun begins to move higher in the sky. To put it another way, the nutrients in the plant compost will no longer be adequate to nourish the plant properly when the growing season begins again.

What applies to a plant in a flowerpot also applies to plants in the closed system of an aquarium: the nutrients get used up. This means giving some thought to a nutrient supply for the plants

This is how to plant. The growth point of the plant should lie just above the level of the substrate, as shown in the lower illustration!

when you are setting up the aquarium and inserting a special **controlled-release fertilizer** for aquarium plants.

If plant growth still seems to be at a standstill, try inserting doses of fertilizer directly around the rootstock. Two or three halved **fertilizer tablets** for aquarium plants should be pushed directly into the substrate, right beside the rootstocks.

In order to prevent damage to sensitive plants, e.g. *Cryptocoryne* spp., you can cover individual tablets with a ball of loam or clay. As soon as the clay (obtainable from pottery or art suppliers) has dried out you can sink the balls into the substrate. The composition of each fertilizer is different and every plant species will require its own individual mixture, so you will have to experiment to find out which preparation is suitable for your plants.

Two tried and tested devices for cleaning the glass panels. Left: A magnetic glass-cleaner which can clean both sides of the glass at the same time. Right: A traditional wiper-blade cleaner.

The best supply of nutrients will not be of much help if the process of photosynthesis – the building of chemical compounds through the influence of light – is unable to function properly. It is therefore vital to have the **correct lighting** above the aquarium because this acts as the plants' energy source.

Plants on a windowsill absorb the **carbon dioxide** necessary for photosynthesis directly from the air so there are seldom any problems. This process is less straightforward in water because various substances contained in the water tend to bind carbon dioxide. This is why 'reinforcements' have to be provided by partial water changes, although the carbon dioxide in tapwater is only available in the short-term. The fish also produce the gas by breathing.

Accessory equipment

Various devices are necessary to ensure that your aquarium functions properly. Most importantly, you must always check the water temperature regularly. The gradations and figures on conventional glass thermometers are very difficult to read at certain angles, especially if they are in a tank! Nowadays, you can buy adhesive **temperature-sensitive strips** which can be attached to the outside of the tank. These are both cheaper and easier to read.

Two devices are useful for cleaning the glass panels: a **magnetic glass-cleaner**, which can remain inside the aquarium, and a **wiper-blade cleaner** for removing occasional stubborn algae. The cleaning surface of the magnetic cleaner is quite abrasive, so it is advisable to wrap it in a thin layer of cotton fabric to avoid scratching the glass if small particles of gravel or sand get caught under it.

The growth of algae on the front panel merely proves that algae are always present. The only important thing is to keep them in check – they will always occur in an illuminated aquarium.

A pair of **plant tongs** for inserting aquarium plants, among other things, as well as an old pair of **paper-scissors** for trimming the leaves and shoots of plants, will make these tasks much easier.

You will also need a special **net** for catching the fish. Nets should have a flexible handle made of plastic-coated wire so that you can reach around corners if necessary.

A **quarantine tank**, made of plastic and holding a few litres (about 4 pt) may be useful for isolating sick fish or providing a short-term refuge for young fish from predatory fish. A **breeding trap** hung over the side of the aquarium will provide a safe haven for the offspring of live-bearing fish, e.g. guppies (*Poecilia reticulata*).

Whether or not you have a hood for your aquarium, you still need a pane of glass or plastic to cover it. This should be placed flat across the aquarium and will both protect the contents of the aquarium and prevent any light fittings in the hood being splashed with water. You can order a pane of glass from a glazier, who should cut out small pieces at one corner to accommodate tubing and cables. The pane should also have a small hole at one end through which to feed the fish. This can be covered with a separate piece of glass. The best plan is to draw a sketch of your requirements, with all the relevant measurements, for the glazier.

A little lemon juice or vinegar solution can be used for cleaning the cover panels but this should be done away from the aquarium and the glass should be wiped off carefully before it is replaced.

A thermometer or an adhesive temperature-sensitive strip can be fixed to the outside of a panel of the aquarium.

Useful accessories for the aquarist. Top: Planting tongs. Bottom: Two sizes of net.

23

Opposite: Black phantom tetras (Megalamphodus megalopterus).

Practical strip battens for supporting the glass cover of an aquarium. Small corners cut out of the glass are necessary for conducting cables and hoses into the tank.

An old pair of paperscissors can be used for shortening or cutting off plant shoots and leaves.

Sick fish and sick aquarium plants

Fish may become ill, even in an aquarium. The introduction of new fish that are already sick, or even contaminated live food, may result in an infection of hitherto healthy fish. It is a good idea to see whether you can avoid using this type of food altogether and, instead, use deep-frozen or dry food to extend their menu.

New fish should never be purchased unless they have been thoroughly checked beforehand. The best plan is to observe them carefully at the retailer's premises, checking, for example, whether their fins are moving properly or are frayed, or if their bodies display flesh-coloured or white patches.

Another warning sign is the presence of dead fish in the retailer's tanks, in which case it might be a good idea to go elsewhere or put off buying any fish for the time being. This care and attention is essential as the damage to your own fish stock at home could otherwise be considerable.

One particular disease (**ichthyophthiriasis**, or 'ich' for short), characterized by white spots, can spread like wildfire and kill off the entire stock in an aquarium. This parasitic illness, which spreads through the water, is sometimes simply called 'white spot'. Excellent medications have been developed but using them always entails a risk of weakening individual fish and plants.

Other diseases may be less harmful and also rarer. Once a correct diagnosis has been made, you will find that relevant medication is available. Poor-quality water can also trigger problems, e.g. **fungal infections**, which create a cottonwool-like appearance on the fish's body. If disease is suspected, the affected fish should immediately be transferred to a quarantine tank and, once a diagnosis has been made – a veterinarian, your local aquarist store or other experienced aquarists may advise you on this – the correct treatment can be implemented.

Plants can suffer from disturbances in their metabolism, or problems due to unfavourable living conditions, e.g. insufficient light. As a result they either do not grow properly or die. Occasionally they suffer from a condition that makes them turn pale. This is generally the result of lack of iron, although sometimes lack of calcium will make the leaves turn yellow. This type of problem can usually be alleviated by employing iron preparations.

A disease that affects *Cryptocoryne*, making the leaves look glassy and become full of holes, or even killing off the entire stock of plants, is caused by sudden changes in water quality, nutrient supply or light levels.

24

Types of aquarium, and suitable fish and plants

The rules of setting up an aquarium with all the necessary equipment have been discussed above. This section covers different types of aquarium and the appropriate fish and plants to buy.

The aquarist trade offers a vast choice of technical equipment, and a glittering and confusing multitude of fish and plants. You will be able to choose from several hundreds of species of tropical fish and more than 200 different plants. Nearly all species are generally robust and adaptable. Only occasionally will you come across sensitive species that have been taken from the wild.

It is, therefore, not a difficult matter to keep aquarium fish and plants in your own home. Once you have ascertained how all the technical devices work, maintaining your aquarium will be quite straightforward. The technical equipment described here has been tried and tested and should work perfectly for many years.

As the confined living space of an aquarium can in no way be compared to a natural habitat, your choice of fish and plants will be based only on their behaviour and living requirements, not on any geographical considerations. This approach has led to the type of aquarium, known as a 'community aquarium', which can accommodate species from different continents.

Opposite Top: *Red-nosed tetra (Hemigrammus rhodostomus).* Bottom: *A cichlid,* Tropheus duboisi, *originating from Lake Tanganyika.*

Above: *A cichlid,* Pseudotropheus lombardoi: *a male is shown here.*

A few species in small groups is preferable.

27

Community aquarium

In this type of aquarium, fish and plants that can live in harmony with each other are put together. There is no sense in putting predatory fish with peaceful species, even if they do originate from the same types of waters, e.g. a combination of piranhas (*Pygocentrus piraya*) and small tetras (e.g. *Hyphessobrycon* spp.) would not work at all. A clear distinction should always be made between the 'bullies' and the more peaceable fish.

The retailer will be unable to gauge what kind of situation awaits the fish in your aquarium, so sometimes you will learn most by your own failures and bitter experience. Ask about compatibility if you are in any doubt. The same goes for the numbers of fish you decide to stock in your aquarium.

Fewer species in small shoals are much more interesting than a large number of many different species.

For the community aquarium, choose fish according to their natural habitat, e.g. small **Corydoras catfish** (*Corydoras* spp.) are suitable for the niche on the floor of the aquarium, where they will take care of left-over food and root about on the bottom.

In principle, they go well with algae-eating fish, which tend to occupy all levels of the aquarium, where they browse on the plants and the decorative elements in the tank while not turning up their noses at meat-rich fish-food. The **Siamese flying fox** (*Epalzeorhynchus siamensis*) or **dwarf sucker catfish** (*Otocinclus affinis*), for example, can be employed as 'cleaners'.

You could also add a **dwarf kribensis**, or **rainbow cichlid**, e.g. *Pelvicachromis pulcher*, to enrich the lower level of the tank. One male and two to three females would be sufficient for a tank of about 100 l (20 gall) capacity.

The middle level is suited to colonization by live-bearers of the family Poeciliidae, e.g. **guppies** (*Poecilia reticulata*) and their close relatives, e.g. the **black molly** (*Poecilia sphenops*) and **sailfin molly** (*Poecilia latipinna*).

As the term 'live-bearer' suggests, such fish produce live offspring. Compared with the offspring of egg-laying tropical fish, the young are relatively large at birth, independently viable

A female of the auratus cichlid (Melanochromis auratus).

from the moment of birth, and are simply the ideal fish for beginners.

The many colour and shape variants of the **swordtail** (*Xiphophorus helleri*) and the related **platy** (*Xiphophorus maculatus*) will also fit well in this fish community.

The region immediately below the water surface is suitable for labyrinth fish (Anabantidae). These species, e.g. the **lace gourami** (*Trichogaster leeri*) and **dwarf gourami** (*Colisa lalia*), are able to absorb oxygen not only from the water but also from the air. The **Siamese fighting fish** (*Betta splendens*), which are often kept in small tanks in aquarist stores, are also members of the family Anabantidae. They are not aggressive towards other fish, but the males must be kept apart. For reproduction purposes, the majority of labyrinth fish build foam nests of air bubbles in which the eggs are laid. These float on the surface and are reinforced with small particles of plant debris.

In a community aquarium, another alternative to labyrinth fish is the well-known **angelfish** (*Pterophyllum* spp.). These are relatively tranquil fish that do, however, grow to be quite large and may then eat their smaller companions. Angelfish should, therefore, be introduced as young fish and may need to be moved to

separate accommodation as they grow larger. Note that their long, trailing fins may be nipped by some fish.

Another South American cichlid is the stunning **discus** (*Symphysodon aequifasciata*), a fish that grows even larger but is quite sensitive to water quality. It is not suitable for a community aquarium, should preferably be kept alone, and is only recommended for experienced aquarists.

You will experience few problems in choosing plants for a community aquarium. Any plant that will thrive in the existing water conditions can be used. In particular, those that produce lots of shoots – 'stalky' plants – are ideal for providing a green background because they can be cut back time and again. Species of *Hygrophila*, e.g. *H. polysperma* and **water wisteria** (*H. difformis*), are particularly recommended.

Ludwigia spp. and **water lobelias** (*Lobelia* spp.), as well as **water hyssop** (*Bacopa* spp.) and **mud plantain** (*Heteranthera zosterifolia*) make good background plants. Stalky plants with a reddish-brown colouring, e.g. like **Joseph's coat** (*Alternanthera* spp.) and *Ammannia* spp., can be placed as solitary plants in front of a different-coloured background.

The middle foreground region, which is the visual centre of the

*A female kribensis, or rainbow cichlid (*Pelvicachromis pulcher*).*

Solitary plants make an eye-catching feature.

aquarium, should be stocked with mainly rosette-shaped, conspicuously coloured plants, e.g. the medium-sized to large Amazon swordplants (*Echinodorus* spp.). Some species of so-called 'aquatic fern' also make ideal solitary plants for this region. These plants are among the most undemanding of all aquarium vegetation and will grow in almost any kind of water, as well as multiplying rapidly by means of the small daughter-plants on their leaves. They include the relatively fine-leaved **Sumatra fern** (*Ceratopteris thalictroides*) and the rather coarse-leaved **Java fern** (*Microsorium pteropus*). Because of their abundant growth you will probably have to replace the mother-plants with smaller shoots now and again.

Both these species can be very useful in an aquarium in which previous attempts at keeping other plants may have failed. Ground-cover plants that grow to only a few centimetres high, e.g. **dwarf arrowhead** (*Sagittaria subulata* var. *pusilla*), provide an attractive finish to the foreground.

Two possibilities for plant aquariums. Top: The flowers of aquarium plants can be observed in open aquariums. Bottom: Fast-growing plants should be placed in aquariums stocked with perch.

Dutch plant aquarium

Using a well-thought out selection of plants in the right arrangement, you could successfully create a Dutch plant aquarium. This type of aquarium is considered to be the epitome of a species-rich planting and requires intensive care. Here, sprouting plants are used not only for the background but also to form a 'street' of plants, with various lengths of stalks, that will require constant replanting.

The aquarium is so densely planted that the bottom is no longer visible. All the plants are graded and matched according to their colour and appearance. This type of aquarium was so-called in honour of the Dutch aquarium enthusiasts who first created this type of planting.

Open aquarium

An aquarium can be kept without a cover as long as the sources of illumination are suspended up at the correct height above it. Because the surface of the water is not covered up, this is called an 'open' aquarium. However, the water will evaporate quickly, raising the relative

Top: *Tiger barb* (Barbus tetrazona). Bottom: *Lace gourami* (Trichogaster leeri).

*A shoal of cardinal tetras (*Cheirodon axelrodi*).*

humidity in the room, and will have to be replaced.

In this, the plants – many of which live partially above the water in the wild – can be observed growing beyond the confines of the aquarium. The formation of flowers and fruit provides an interesting dimension to plant care.

The enthusiast may attempt to grow some of the aquarium plants, e.g. **Amazon swordplants** (*Echinodorus* spp.), from seed.

By surrounding the aquarium with glass, you can create a micro-climate with a high relative humidity and thus turn an open aquarium into an entire 'river-bank' or 'vivarium'. However, with this type of aquarium, you should remember that many species of fish are capable of jumping right out of the water. To avoid any

accidents make sure you choose fish which are suited to this kind of arrangement.

Red phantom tetras (Megalamphodus sweglesi).

Shoal aquarium

If you are not keen on the colourful mixture in a community or open aquarium, you may choose to concentrate on just a few species of fish and set up a shoal aquarium.

The emphasis in this type of aquarium is on fish that live in shoals. To enable typical shoaling behaviour to take place in an aquarium means bearing the following points in mind:

- The tank should be long rather than tall.
- Never introduce any fish that will chase the members of a shoal.

35

A colour variant of the zebra mbuna (Pseudo-tropheus zebra).

Tetras, e.g. the widely available **cardinal tetra** (*Paracheirodon axelrodi*) or the **red phantom tetra** (*Megalamphodus sweglesi*), are ideal shoal fish.

The group dynamics of the shoal will only be displayed, however, if the fish are present in sufficient numbers. As many species tend to be rather small, a good dozen or more individuals should be introduced. The remainder of the fish stock can consist of those species familiar from the community aquarium.

Other families of fish that also live in shoals may be considerably more aggressive than tetras. This applies to fish of the carp family, e.g. the **tiger barb** (*Barbus tetrazona*), and the **zebra barb** (*Barbus eugrammus*). Because these species are so voracious they may occasionally resort to attacking other fish, particularly their fins. This will tend to be the case if the other fish have thread-like pelvic fins, e.g. the angelfish (*Pterophyllum* spp.). This means experimenting with different species of fish to determine which can be kept with them in an aquarium. The algae-eating fish, e.g. the Siamese flying fox (*Epalzeorhynchus siamensis*), are likely candidates.

Plants should be arranged to form a dense background with plenty of swimming space in the foreground. Solitary, flat-growing plants, e.g. medium-sized **Amazon swordplants** (*Echinodorus* spp.), can be grown here and will proliferate well via their shoots.

Species aquarium

Cichlids are considered to be rather tough characters with respect to getting on with other aquarium inhabitants and really require an aquarium to themselves.

With the exception of the dwarf varieties, cichlids grow relatively large compared with other tropical fish. Their wide range of colouring extends from lightest yellow to brightest cherry red and, in this respect, they compare favourably with coral-reef fish from tropical waters.

In addition to their splendid colouring, their reproductive behaviour is also particularly interesting. Some species hide their spawn in caves or raise their fry in specially dug trenches. After the young fish have hatched, they are cared for and defended against predators to the point of self-sacrifice.

Because of this extraordinary reproductive behaviour (by comparison, (for example, tetras, for example, allow their eggs to fall into the water and will often later eat them) and the intensive care of the offspring, many cichlids need places where they can hide their young. This requirement has led to the evolution of true specialists.

Numerous species occupy small territories between rock clefts or stones. This kind of behaviour is particularly pronounced in many cichlids from East African lakes. Others will lay their eggs in

A platy (Xiphophorus maculatus) with dark tail fins.

The behaviours described require the installation of well-thought-out decoration and planting in the tank because cichlids may be purely vegetarian as well as carnivorous.

empty snail shells. Cichlids that live in habitats with a sandy bottom, e.g. in Central or South American rivers, dig spawning pits in the substrate. Many species also utilize stones or leaves as a medium for depositing spawn.

During the course of evolution, some species of cichlids obviously had none of these niches for depositing spawn at their disposal so their mouths became adapted for use as a 'breeding cavity'.

Dwarf cichlids, which are generally less than 10 cm (4 in) long, show similar types of behaviour to large cichlids, and are therefore particularly suitable as ornamental fish. A half-broken flowerpot, half a coconut shell or a similar 'cave' placed at their disposal will make them peaceable inhabitants of an aquarium, although they will not be able to stand up to larger cichlids.

As a rule, robust, fast-growing aquarium plants can be used. Large, sturdy plants, e.g. the **Amazon swordplan**t (*Echi-nodorus parviflorus*), are particularly suitable. To protect the rootstock and help maintain these plants, place a ring of stones around their base.

Resistant plants that derive their nutrients mainly from the water, e.g. **Anubias** spp. or **Java fern** (*Microsorium pteropus*), can be protected well by tree roots. For this purpose, use a wood drill

The zebra danio (Brachydanio rerio) lives together well in a shoal.

Opposite: Top: *Tanganyikan golden cichlid (Lamprologus leleupi) is counted among the relatively peaceable cichlids.* Bottom: *The platy (Xiphophorus maculatus).*

39

to bore holes 2 cm (³/₄ in) deep in the tree roots and insert the plants, with their rootstocks, into these holes.

Open areas of pebbles for digging in should also be offered, as well as stones which can be used as hiding places and territorial markers.

If you wish to avoid damage to your plants or fish, you should remember, if you buy cichlids, that the morning after placing them in the tank, you may find the plants floating on the surface or completely eaten. On the other hand, experienced cichlid enthusiasts report having success even with the very sensitive *Cryptocoryne* as many cichlids obviously do not like the taste of these plants. Nevertheless, cichlids add more life and interest to an aquarium than probably any other family of fish.

Naturally, you can also set up a species aquarium for other species or families of fish. This is almost always done with thoughts of breeding in mind, although some fish, even some cichlids, have specific water-quality needs which cannot be met in an ordinary community aquarium.

Breeding aquarium

Successful breeding depends not only on having a pair of fish, but also on the quality of the water. For example, many **dwarf cichlids** from South America require very soft water, while those from Africa will only reproduce in hard water.

Tetras (*Hyphessobrycon* spp.) on the other hand, as well as certain water conditions, will require dense plant growth on the bottom, e.g. **Java moss** (*Vesicularia dubyana*). Here, the eggs, and later the fry can develop in protected conditions, as tetras – like live-bearing fish – are 'bad' parents and tend to eat their offspring.

A breeding-trap in which eggs and fry can safely grow.

40

Plants with floating leaves are especially suitable for **labyrinth fish**, which like to hover beneath them. Floating plants on the surface of the water can also be a source of building material for the fish.

There is no need for any other special decoration for breeding aquariums as they are used for only one purpose.

Habitat aquarium

In order to offer their tropical fish something really special, enthusiasts often have the idea of setting up a habitat aquarium. What they do not seem to realize is that the original natural environment of fish can never be completely recaptured in an aquarium. The only thing you can do is install relevant furnishings.

For example, a habitat aquarium stocked with **neon tetras** (*Paracheirodon innesi*) from South America should have layers of dead vegetable matter lying on the bottom.

For **labyrinth fish**, **rice plants** (*Oryza* spp.) should be growing out of the aquarium and for **angelfish** (*Pterophyllum* spp.) lots of thin twigs or roots should be inserted in the substrate.

Therefore, in trying to provide your fish with an environment that is as natural as possible, your aquarium will not be so attractive to look at.

The marbled variety of Hygrophila polysperma.

Opposite: Top left: *Joseph's coat* (Alternanthera *spp.*). Top right: Ammannia *spp.* Centre left: *Water hyssop* (Bacopa *spp.*). Centre right: *Amazon swordplant* (Echinodorus parviflorus). Bottom left: Anubias *spp.* Bottom right: *Sumatra fern* (Ceratopteris thalictroides).

Top: *Water lobelias* (Lobelia *spp.*). Centre: *Wendt's cryptocoryne* (Cryptocoryne wendtii). Bottom: *Water wisteria* (Hygrophila difformis).

*Dwarf arrowhead
(Sagittaria subulata var.
pusilla)*

To cover all the types of special aquariums, and the instructions for setting up and maintaining them, would be an extremely lengthy task. For information on the different fish groups, e.g. labyrinth fish, tetras, catfish, cichlids, and even aquarium plants, you should refer to the specialist literature and societies which deal exclusively with a particular subject.

What I am trying to indicate above is that sooner or later, even a beginner may wish to decide in which direction he or she would like to specialize. Collecting a colourful range of tropical fish species in the limited confines of a community aquarium often proves disastrous because none of the fish feels really at home. Susceptibility to disease is increased and the chances of breeding – the crowning achievement of this hobby – are almost non-existent. The care and breeding of tropical fish and aquarium plants offer many other possibilities, which is why this wonderful hobby is so popular and aquarists have so much to talk about.

There are a multitude of opportunities for specialization within this hobby. Those who choose not to take advantage of them will remain eternal beginners.

Index

Picture sources
Photographs on pages 1, 25, 26 (2), 27, 29, 30, 31, 33 (2), 34, 35, 36, 37, 38 (2),
39, 41 and 42 (2) are by Regina Kuhn. Those on pages 2–3, 4, 6, 7, 8, 11, 12, 13,
15, 16, 43, 44 (6), 45 (3) and 46 are by Bernd Greger. Black-and-white illustrations
are by Siegfried Lokau, of Bochum-Wattenscheid, as commissioned by the publishers.

Acknowledgements
Thanks for their support and help in preparing this volume go to the following firms:
Gröger Cichlid Centre and the Märkischer Zoo Butzkamm, both in Berlin, as well as to
Zoo-Utke, Esslingen, and Kolle-Zoo, Stuttgart.

A BLANDFORD BOOK
First published in the UK 1997 by Blandford
A Cassell imprint
Cassell plc
Wellington House 125 Strand London WC2R 0BB

Text copyright © 1997 Cassell plc
Translated by Astrid Mick
Originally published as *Fische* by Bernd Greger
World copyright © Eugen Ulmer GmbH & Co., Stuttgart,Germany

Distributed in the United States by Sterling Publishing Co., Inc.,
387 Park Avenue South, New York, NY 10016-8810

A Cataloguing-in-Publication Data entry for this title is available from the British
Library

ISBN 0-7137-2684-9

Printed and bound in Spain